F R A N K
L L O Y D
W R I G H T
W E S T
P O R T F O L I O

Text & Photographs by
Thomas A. Heinz

GIBBS·SMITH
PUBLISHER

To Randell Makinson, Director Emeritus of the Gamble House in Pasadena, for the many years of friendship and insightful architectural discussions that have never become too academic, never boring, and are, in fact, inspiring.

DF AB EW EA∞

First Edition

97 96 95 94 8 7 6 5 4 3 2 1

Text and photographs copyright © 1994 by Thomas A. Heinz

This is a Peregrine Smith Book, published by
Gibbs Smith, Publisher
P.O. Box 667
Layton, Utah 84041

Cover photograph: Marin County Building, West Elevation, © 1994 by Thomas A. Heinz
Design by J. Scott Knudsen, Park City, Utah
Printed by Regent Publishing Services, Hong Kong

Library of Congress Cataloging–in–Publication Data

Heinz, Thomas A.
    Frank Lloyd Wright portfolio. West/Thomas A. Heinz.
      p.   cm.
    ISBN 0-87905-599-5
    1. Architecture—West (U.S.) 2. Architecture, Modern—20th century—United States.
3. Wright, Frank Lloyd, 1867-1959—Themes, motives.   I. Title.
NA725.H54 1994
720 '.92—dc20   93-29287
                                                          CIP

FRANK LLOYD WRIGHT ADMIRED Japanese buildings because they appeared to be a natural outgrowth of their site. The colors and textures of the wooden frames and the straw plaster walls were expressions of man artfully working with nature in an organic harmony.

Especially in the West, Wright made an effort to use local materials. His earliest building on the West Coast was constructed before 1910, and he built in the West during every decade after that time until his death nearly fifty years later. The buildings in this area are the most unique and varied of any other grouping of his work. The climates Wright built in include deserts, mountains, and lush valleys. Those built in earthquake zones, such as the Imperial Hotel in Tokyo and the Millard House in Pasadena, fared better than most people expected and are excellent examples of earthquake-resistant construction.

Wright's ability to select materials appropriate to each environment is exemplary. In the case of Taliesin West, desert rock is artistically arranged in the walls of the structure, making it literally a growth from its site. Wood frames are anchored to these rock walls and span the walls much like trees. Canvas roofs with interior gutters allow the water to drain on the inside, making it possible to control its entry points and flow. The California concrete-block houses use a decomposed granite found on the sites of the buildings themselves.

From time to time, the buildings are restored, refurbished, or otherwise altered by their owners. Many of the owners, both public and private, are seeing the advantages and beauty of Wright's original designs and are restoring as best they can with the money available. They are uncovering many secrets that the buildings hold and those little discussed by Wright. The restoration at the Barnsdall "Hollyhock" House is worth mentioning here: two couches—the largest pieces of free-standing furniture ever designed by Wright—have transformed the space, and an original color scheme is being introduced through research findings. If you haven't seen the house since 1989, please return for a new experience.

Thomas A. Heinz
Millard House, Pasadena,
June 1992

IMPERIAL HOTEL
NORTH ELEVATION

This is the reconstruction of the central pavilion of the hotel. It retains the color, texture, scale, and details of the original. One side is reconstructed of the original materials and the other of new mixed with original. The complexity of the spaces is unexpected, as is the richness of the detail. Nearly everything is ornamented—*textured* might be a more appropriate term, because it is not overwhelming or gauche. As in nature, all of the parts are in harmony.

IMPERIAL HOTEL
REFLECTING POOL SPRITE

Several Wright buildings incorporate sculpture. Wright's own studio starts the list, which continues with Dana House, Bogk House, Midway Gardens, Barnsdall House, and ends with the Nakoma-Nakomis sculptures in the Madison Project for a golf course. In the Imperial Hotel example, there is no artistic collaborator of record as with other Wright-designed sculptures. The abstraction has neither an oriental nor an American influence, but it blends pleasingly with the environment of the hotel. It is only after a second look that one notices it is a human form.

GAKUEN SCHOOL
SOUTH ELEVATION

The basic plan is similar to that of the Imperial Hotel, with a central pavilion and symmetrical wings. The continuance of the school is now threatened because it occupies a very valuable piece of land, worth an estimated $300 million. The school is still in operation. All of the simple Wright-designed wood tables and chairs are in daily use.

ALINE BARNSDALL HOUSE
"HOLLYHOCK HOUSE"
WEST ELEVATION

*I*n the set of original drawings, there are three schemes for this facade. They clearly show a transition from Prairie School into the abstract. The Prairie scheme was complete with low-pitched overhanging roof to be done in red tile. The house sits on top of a hill that was originally part of an olive grove and is known as Olive Hill. Wright's son, Lloyd, assisted his father in the construction of this and other Los Angeles projects.

ALINE BARNSDALL HOUSE
"HOLLYHOCK HOUSE"
WEST PIER

When the house was built, Los Angeles was still considered an arid location. Those few windows in the house are deeply inset to help shield the interior from the harsh desert sun. The walls are constructed of lath and stucco overlaying wood studs.

ALINE BARNSDALL HOUSE "HOLLYHOCK HOUSE" POOL AND COURTYARD

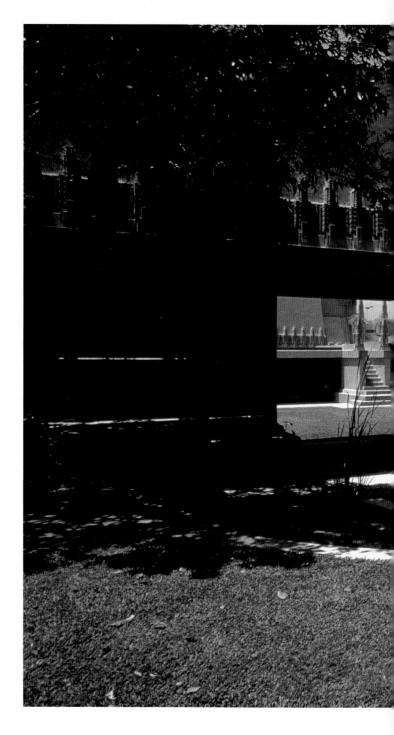

T he original courtyard had a stream that ran from the pond in the courtyard toward the living room, where it disappeared underground. It reappeared in a pond in front of the living-room fireplace and finally ended in another pond on the west front (see page 11). This was certainly to be considered an oasis and was a way to cool the air in the courtyard, which in turn would help cool the house. A small bronze statue stood in the center under the bridge.

ALINE BARNSDALL HOUSE
"HOLLYHOCK HOUSE"
COURTYARD PIER

The hollyhock is the design motif for the house. All hollyhock motifs used in this house are based on the same design. They are more, or in some instances, less elaborate in the capitals, along the base of the mansard, along the front and sides of the house, and in the front columns. Colorful hollyhocks grow in the gardens. It has been said that the hollyhock was a favorite flower of Aline Barnsdall.

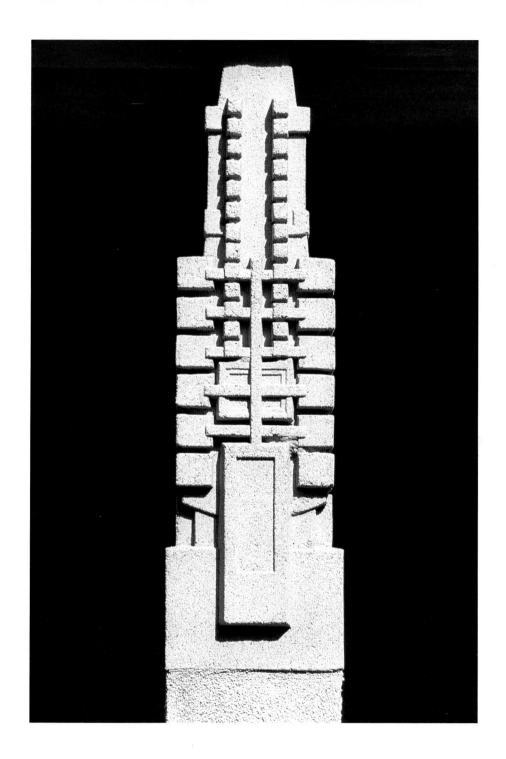

SAMUEL FREEMAN HOUSE
LIVING ROOM

The furniture shown here in the living room of the Freeman House was designed by a former employee of Wright's, Rudolph Schindler, who went on to become a renowned architect. The original Wright designs consisted of two high-backed wood benches flanking the fireplace. There were even taller bookcases outside the benches against the wall. The coffee table between the benches was cut down from the original dining table soon after it was built. The look of the Schindler scheme is much less formal than Wright's benches suggest.

SAMUEL FREEMAN HOUSE
CONCRETE BLOCK

All of the blocks used in the Freeman House are sixteen inches square on the face, the same dimension as all of the Los Angeles block houses. The pattern includes an abstraction of a tulip, perhaps a favorite of the Freemans. Other patterned blocks were pierced and used as light-screen windows in the clerestory above the benches and occasionally in the walls. The pierced blocks had the deepest recesses removed and plate glass was set between the inner and outer blocks to become a weather barrier.

JOHN STORER HOUSE
CONCRETE BLOCK

The Storer House utilizes many styles of patterned blocks. They are simpler patterns than on either the Freeman or the Ennis houses. The present owner discovered the forms, and new blocks have been carefully made to replace the many blocks that have been damaged or have deteriorated over the past sixty years. The forms are made of aluminum, and the aggregate is decomposed granite found on the site. The blocks are made by hand with a very dry cement mix.

CHARLES ENNIS HOUSE
SOUTH ELEVATION

The Ennis House is a large, one-bedroom structure. The master bedroom is located at the extreme right. The building is sited along the top of a ridge near the Greek Theatre and the Griffith Observatory. It is directly north of the Hollyhock House, and one house can be seen from the other. The Ennis House has been seen in many movies and commercial advertisements. It has been the site of numerous weddings, even though there is very little on-site parking and virtually no street parking.

CHARLES ENNIS HOUSE
SOUTH ELEVATION, DETAIL

Many years ago an owner who has long since passed away decided to put a rubber coating on the blocks to prevent water from seeping through the blocks or the joints between them. Needless to say, this coating has deteriorated and is in need of work; solutions are still being sought. The outside garden, located just behind this wall, has been restored. It is overlooked by the bedroom on the right and the library on the left.

Charles Ennis House
Dining Room Piers

This ornamental archway separates the dining room from the entry stair and hallway. It is composed of a set of stacked corner blocks. It appears to be only ornamental, but it actually helps to transfer the load between the interior walls during the many earthquakes in the area. Because of this and the steel that is placed in the horizontal and vertical joints, called knitlock, the house has suffered minimal damage over the past seventy years.

CHARLES ENNIS HOUSE
CONCRETE BLOCK

The most highly detailed of the California blocks, these were also handmade in aluminum molds. Decomposed granite on this hill served as the concrete aggregate. There were two other buildings constructed of concrete blocks before the Usonian period: the Arizona Biltmore Hotel and a house in Tulsa for Wright's cousin, Richard Lloyd Jones. Wright was not one to throw away a good idea and proposed owner-made concrete-block houses that were termed Usonian Automatic. It is unclear what the automatic part was intended to be, but several were built. The most outstanding example is in St. Louis.

ARIZONA BILTMORE HOTEL
EAST FACADE

Although former employee Albert McArthur is the architect of record, Wright's influence in the design is unmistakable. The blocks are not square, as in the Los Angeles houses and as Wright originally intended. White milk-glass blocks are used in certain areas; with light bulbs behind them, they provide soft illumination. The knitlock system was developed by Wright in the Los Angeles houses earlier in the 1920s. Two Wright-designed houses lie on adjacent lots just to the east: the Adelman and the Boomer houses, built in the 1950s. The legend goes that Mr. Adelman and his friends would walk over to the Biltmore nearly every day for lunch and a game of cards.

ARIZONA BILTMORE HOTEL LOBBY

T he darkness makes the lobby exude a feeling of coolness, so it becomes a retreat from the intense Phoenix sun. The black lacquered table with red edges in the center of the lobby is an adaptation of one located in the drafting room at Hillside in Spring Green. The ceiling is real gold leaf, installed the old-fashioned way—one four-inch sheet at a time. After a devastating fire several years ago, Taliesin Associated Architects restored the hotel in record time— over the summer, ready for the opening of the winter tourist season.

ARIZONA BILTMORE HOTEL
WALL DETAIL

T he block pattern was sculpted by Emry Kopta, from Austria, who also assisted Wright with the San Marcos in the Desert Project. Rather than carve out deep areas in the pattern and place a light bulb behind for illumination, at the Biltmore blocks were cast in white milk glass in the same pattern as the solid concrete units. The pattern is invisible at night, and the blocks appear to be white areas of light.

TALIESIN WEST
SOUTH ELEVATION

Frank Lloyd Wright was stricken with pneumonia in the late 1930s. His doctor advised him to get out of the cold and damp Wisconsin winter and go to a warmer, drier climate. Wright chose a sloping site way out in the desert twenty-five miles east and north of downtown Phoenix. In the early years there were few roads and one could travel across the desert floor. Today the house is more difficult to locate. One must look carefully for the red sign and wind through housing developments up to the entry gate. The Salt Creek Canal and an annoying high-voltage line must be traversed before entering the tranquil compound. There is no mistaking it once you arrive. Wright was able to tame the wild desert and make it serve the needs of himself and the Fellowship.

TALIESIN WEST
DRAFTING ROOM ENTRY

Often referred to as Camp, the temporary appearance of the original materials was well suited to the desert. The original roof was white canvas attached to redwood frames. The bright orange plywood doors remain, perhaps as a reminder of those days. These materials have been replaced by steel sections and fiberglass. The enclosed space is now air-conditioned for year-round use. A petroglyph on the large rock is a reminder of the many peoples who have occupied these lands.

JEAN AND PAUL HANNA HOUSE
SOUTH ELEVATION

T he Hannas were both school-teachers. Paul Hanna was also the social studies editor of the *World Book Encyclopedia* for thirty-five years. Unable to find a contractor who could understand Wright's design, the Hannas acted as their own contractor. Much of the furniture was hand-built by Paul in his home workshop.

JEAN AND PAUL HANNA HOUSE
DINING ROOM ELEVATION

With much foresight, the Hannas directed Wright to design their house so it could be modified as their needs changed over the years. The original playroom later became a more formal dining room. The children's bedrooms were reconfigured and became the office for both Hannas. The house was given to Stanford University as a residence for exceptional visiting scholars.

GEORGE D. STURGES HOUSE
LIVING AND DINING ROOM

Much like the Freeman House (page 19), the fireplace and adjacent walls have no windows. The opposite south wall is filled with windows and looks out on a wonderful view of lush rolling hills. The furniture was designed for the house. The armchair on the left is frequently referred to as an origami chair, because it resembles this Japanese form of folded-paper construction.

MORRIS GIFT SHOP
ENTRY ARCH

The interior of the shop is a single large spiral reminiscent of the Guggenheim ramp. The exterior facade, in contrast, is a flat plane of brick. The lack of ornament over such a large surface makes the small building appear larger that its dimensions. The detail of the vertical brick and the thin line of horizontal limestone gently direct the eye to the entrance. At night the lights under the limestone and behind the brick screen accomplish the same. The red square tile bears Wright's signature on this work of art.

PRICE TOWER
ELEVATION

The story of Price Tower is that Mr. Price requested a two-story office building. Frank Lloyd Wright responded that three stories were more economical. Later, they compromised on a nineteen-story office and apartment building. Price must have been pleased with the outcome, because he later commissioned two houses—one in Bartelsville and the other in Phoenix. The tower itself is a statement in organic design. Since each side has a different orientation to the sun and there are offices and apartments, each of the four sides expresses these differences through window position, sunscreen louvers, and balcony location.

PRICE TOWER
COPPER FRIEZE

As in nature, there is something to see, some detail at every level. This is one of the expressions of organic design. The green patina was added to the copper for color. It would have taken many years in this arid location for the water to produce this level of oxidation. The patina also gave it a more even tone than would likely occur naturally; it might have shown streaks. The green also relates to Wright's idea for the structure—a tree on the prairie. At one time, the building could have been seen from quite a distance.

BENJAMIN ADELMAN HOUSE FIREPLACE MURAL

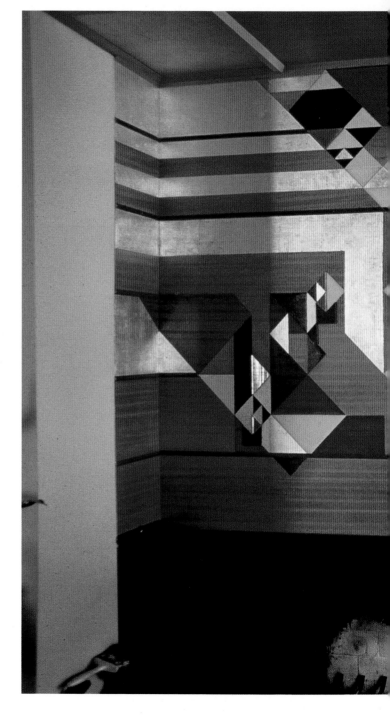

O nly special houses had this kind of decorative element. It is not clear whether the idea came from Wright or from Adelman. Colored and gold paint combined with inlaid glass and contrasting wood stain make up the components of the Adelman mural. The horizontal bands of the concrete block are carried through the design. Mr. and Mrs. Kopulos, recent owners, carefully cleaned it, and they added the swimming pool much later.

DAVID WRIGHT HOUSE
MASTER BEDROOM ELEVATION

Of Wright's four sons, the first two became architects. The youngest became a Washington attorney and David Wright was a representative for a concrete-block manufacturer. The house was constructed on a concrete spiral, with concrete block house added on top of it. Being raised above the ground, the house is better able to catch the desert breezes. And since it sits in an orange grove, beautiful fragrances permeate the home when the hundreds of trees are in bloom.

DAVID WRIGHT HOUSE
LIVING ROOM RUG DETAIL

This original design was made by Frank Lloyd Wright and executed by V'soske, now of Puerto Rico. The Wrights have saved some of the original yarns in a bag in the bottom drawer of a dresser. A comparison of the rug to the stored yarns shows that the rug still retained its original colors. As bold as it appears in this photograph, after being in the room a while, one is not distracted by the colors or pattern.

MARIN COUNTY BUILDING
LIBRARY DOME

Completed after Wright's death, some details were simplified in an effort to save costs, but the basic concept of a Roman aqueduct joining several hills was kept intact. This is the longest of the Wright-designed structures. The domes give the building an exotic appeal. The arches, set away from the wall, keep the sun out of the interior while fascilating great views in all directions.

MARIN COUNTY BUILDING ARCHES

T he Marin County Building looks like it belongs in its setting. No other building would be as harmonious as this is with the site. Even with the repetition of the arches, it is not boring, but would be described as quiet or serene. Sited slightly east of Highway 101, just north of San Francisco, it is likely seen by more people than any other Wright building. Next to it is the only building designed by Frank Lloyd Wright for the federal government—a small post office.

Benjamin Adelman House, 1951
5710 North 30th Street
Phoenix, Arizona
Page 54

❦ Aline Barnsdall House,
  "Hollyhock House," 1920
4800 Hollywood Boulevard
Los Angeles, California
Pages 10,12,14,16

❦ Arizona Biltmore Hotel, 1928
24th Street at Missouri Avenue
Phoenix, Arizona
Pages 32, 34, 36

❦ Charles Ennis House, 1924
2607 Glendower Avenue
Los Angeles, California
Pages 24, 26, 28, 30

Samuel Freeman House, 1924
1962 Glencoe Way
Los Angeles, California
Pages 18, 20

❦ Gakuen School, 1921
31-4 Nishi, Ikebukuro
2-Chrome
Tokyo, Japan
Page 8

Jean and Paul Hanna House,
  1937
737 Frenchman's Way
Stanford, California
Pages 42, 44

❦ Imperial Hotel, 1917
Meiji Mura Park, Inuyama City
near Nagoya Japan
Pages 4, 6

❦ Marin County Building, 1957
U.S. 101 at San Pedro Road
San Raphael, California
Pages 60, 62

❦ Morris Gift Shop, 1948
140 Maiden Lane
San Francisco, California
Page 48

❦ Price Tower, 1952
Dewey Avenue at N.E. 6th
  Street
Bartelsville, Oklahoma
Pages 50, 52

John Storer House, 1923
8161 Hollywood Boulevard
Los Angeles, California
Page 22

George D. Sturges House, 1939
449 Skieway Drive
Brentwood Heights, California
Page 46

❦ Taliesin West, 1938
11000 Shea Boulevard
Scottsdale, Arizona
Pages 38, 40

David Wright House, 1950
5202 East Exeter Boulevard
Phoenix, Arizona
Pages 56, 58

❦ These properties are open for public tours.